THE 12 BIGGEST BREAKTHROUGHS IN
MEDICINE

by M. M. Eboch

www.12StoryLibrary.com

12-Story Library is an imprint of Peterson Publishing Company and Press Room Editions.

Produced for 12-Story Library by Red Line Editorial

Photographs ©: wonderisland/Shutterstock Images, cover, 1; Luis Santos/Shutterstock Images, 4; Vasileios Karafillidis/Shutterstock Images, 5; Dragon Images/Shutterstock Images, 6; vitstudio/Shutterstock Images, 7, 26, 28; yang na/Shutterstock Images, 8; Bettmann/Corbis, 9; Thinkstock, 10; sfam_photo/Shutterstock Images, 11; Shane Maritich/Shutterstock Images, 12; dcwcreations/Shutterstock Images, 13, 15; Tyler Olson/Shutterstock Images, 14, 18; catolla/Shutterstock Images, 16; AP Images, 17, 22; goa novi/Shutterstock Images, 19; Taewafeel/Shutterstock Images, 20; Africa Studio/Shutterstock Images, 21; Hemera Technologies/Thinkstock, 23, 29; Mayovskyy Andrew/Shutterstock Images, 24; Ericsmandes/Shutterstock Images, 25; Peter Macdiarmid/PA Wire/AP Images, 27

ISBN
978-1-63235-015-2 (hardcover)
978-1-63235-075-6 (paperback)
978-1-62143-056-8 (hosted ebook)

Library of Congress Control Number: 2014937358

Printed in the United States of America
Mankato, MN
June, 2014

Go beyond the book. Get free, up-to-date content on this topic at 12StoryLibrary.com.

TABLE OF CONTENTS

HIPPOCRATES INTRODUCES SCIENTIFIC THOUGHT TO MEDICINE

Technology is the use of science to solve problems. We usually think of machines, devices, and cool gadgets as technology. But sometimes it can mean a new way of thinking. Greek physician Hippocrates introduced a new way of thinking about medicine in approximately 430 BCE. At that time, most doctors knew little about disease. They diagnosed diseases based only on what the patient said. Many doctors thought that diseases had supernatural causes. They treated medical problems with prayers and religious sacrifices.

Hippocrates viewed disease and the practice of medicine in a more scientific way. He figured out that a disease could affect the whole body. He thoroughly examined a patient and looked for physical symptoms. Hippocrates also took into account

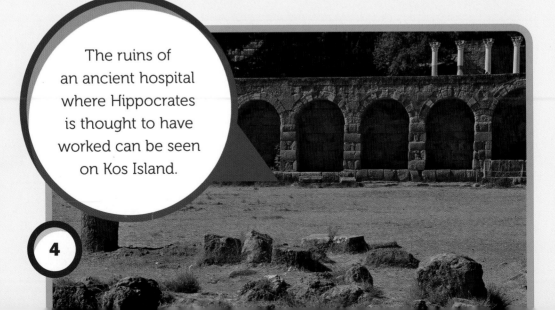

The ruins of an ancient hospital where Hippocrates is thought to have worked can be seen on Kos Island.

the patient's medical history, living conditions, and behaviors. By paying close attention to patients, he learned that some habits and ways of life seemed to lead to certain diseases. He also noticed that some diseases spread through the air and water.

Not all of Hippocrates's ideas turned out to be right. But he is thought to be one of the first doctors to base his practice on scientific study. This is why he became known as the father of medicine.

Hippocrates lived from approximately 460 to 375 BCE.

GALEN

Another Greek doctor, Galen, built on Hippocrates's ideas. Born in 131 CE, Galen was one of the first scientists to study the human body through experiments. He used controlled experiments to study the function of internal organs such as the kidneys. But much of Galen's research was lost. His scientific methods did not start to become common until the 1500s.

60

Number of writings originally credited to Hippocrates. Historians now think some of them were written by other doctors.

- Scientific thought was introduced by Hippocrates in approximately 430 BCE in Greece.
- Diagnosed diseases based on observation and logic.
- Took into account living conditions and behaviors that could cause disease.

2

MICROSCOPE HELPS SCIENTISTS STUDY ANATOMY

Zacharias and Hans Janssen were experimenting with two lenses in a tube in 1597 when they made a discovery. They positioned one lens as an eyepiece and the other close to the object to be viewed. This early attempt at a microscope enlarged the object so that it could be viewed in more detail.

Soon, scientists were using the microscope to study the human body. They could now see aspects of anatomy that had been invisible to the human eye. In 1661, Italian doctor Marcello Malpighi saw tiny blood vessels called capillaries. His observations helped scientists learn how blood moves through the body.

Malpighi and other doctors also studied the liver, brain, kidneys, and other organs using the microscope. Later scientists learned how cells

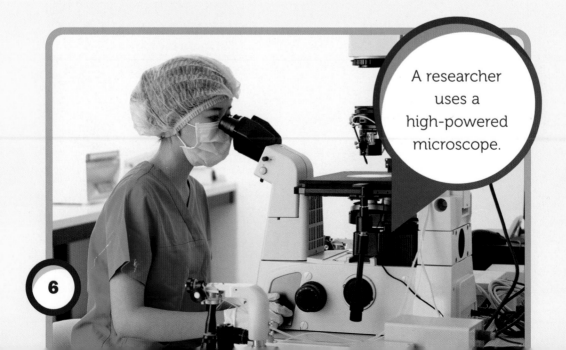

A researcher uses a high-powered microscope.

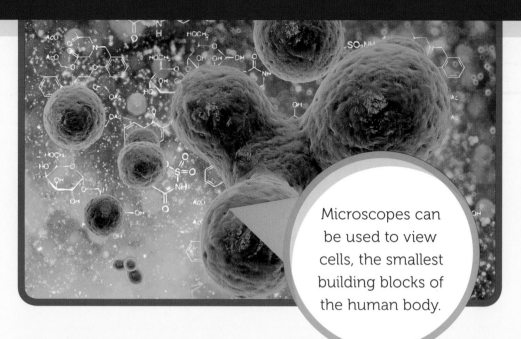

Microscopes can be used to view cells, the smallest building blocks of the human body.

work. They studied bacteria and viruses, tiny organisms that cause many diseases. With microscopes, scientists gained a better understanding of how the body worked. They were able to use that knowledge to learn how to treat it.

STETHOSCOPES

Doctors can also learn from listening to the body. The stethoscope helps doctors listen to the heart and lungs. It was created by a French doctor in 1816. The first stethoscope was a hollow wooden tube. Doctors could use the tube instead of placing their ear directly on a patient's chest. The sound was louder and clearer. Later stethoscopes had rubber tubing. They transmitted sound directly to the doctor's ears.

2,000
Times a compound microscope, which has two lenses, can magnify an object.

- The microscope was invented by Zacharias and Hans Janssen.
- Used to study human anatomy in closer detail.
- Used to learn about viruses and bacteria that cause diseases.
- Led to new ways to diagnose diseases.

SMALLPOX VACCINE ENDS DEADLY DISEASE

The human body has its own way to fight disease. It produces antibodies in response to viruses and bacteria. Vaccines contain a small amount of a virus. The virus is usually in a dead or weakened form. This tricks the body into forming antibodies to fight the virus without making the person sick. If the person is ever exposed to the virus in live form, the body will be ready to fight if off. In most cases, a person who has been vaccinated will not get sick.

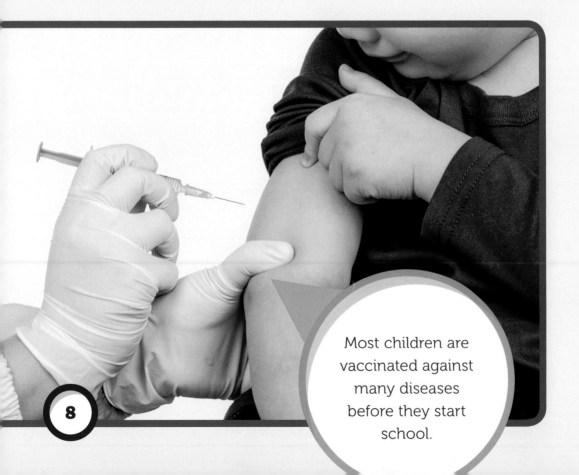

Most children are vaccinated against many diseases before they start school.

A British doctor gives a smallpox vaccination to a boy in 1796.

30
Number of diseases that are prevented by vaccines.

- Edward Jenner introduced the smallpox vaccine in 1796.
- Eliminated smallpox worldwide by 1977.
- Led doctors to develop vaccines for many other serious diseases.

British doctor Edward Jenner made the first vaccine in 1796. It was for smallpox, a serious disease that is fatal in many cases. Jenner noticed that cows became infected with a similar but much less serious virus, cowpox. When he infected a boy with cowpox, the boy got sick. But he quickly recovered. He was then safe from smallpox. This method was soon used all over. Over time, smallpox was wiped out. The last US case was in 1949. The last case in the world was in Africa in 1977.

BETTER ANESTHETICS EASE THE PAIN OF SURGERY

For thousands of years, doctors have used various ways to lessen pain during medical procedures. Early Greek and Arabic doctors may have given patients mind-altering drugs, such as cannabis or opium, before a surgery. Later, British sailors were given strong alcohol before an amputation. These were early forms of anesthetics.

An anesthetic is a drug that causes a person to lose feeling in a part of the body. Surgeons can take the time to work carefully, knowing the patient cannot feel what is happening. An anesthetic also keeps a patient from moving during a procedure.

In 1799, Sir Humphry Davy discovered that nitrous oxide could be used as an anesthetic. It is also known as "laughing gas."

Sir Humphry Davy discovered nitrous oxide could be used as an anesthetic.

15

Seconds it typically takes a patient to become unconscious using modern anesthetics.

- Anesthetics were introduced in the 1940s.
- Discovered by Sir Humphry Davy.
- Lessens pain or causes unconsciousness during medical or dental procedures.

In 1845, dentists started to give nitrous oxide to patients when pulling teeth. Within the next decade, doctors were using ether and chloroform to make patients fully unconscious for surgery. At first, the practice was risky. If too much was given, the drug could make the patient stop breathing. But over time, doctors learned how to correctly measure doses. Safer anesthetics were introduced. Soon, it was common practice to use anesthetics in most surgeries.

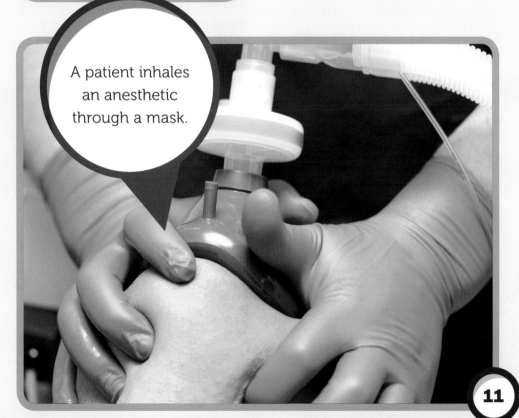

A patient inhales an anesthetic through a mask.

ASPIRIN BECOMES BREAKTHROUGH PAIN RELIEVER

In ancient Greece, Hippocrates gave patients a powder made from the bark of a willow tree. He used it to treat pain and fever. In the 1820s, scientists figured out that the willow bark worked because it contained salicin. They learned how to separate the chemical from the rest of the bark. They used it to make salicylic acid and gave it to patients. It reduced fever and pain, but it also caused stomach problems.

In 1853, a German chemist mixed salicylic acid with other chemicals to make it less acidic. The mixture had fewer side effects. The company Bayer started marketing the pain

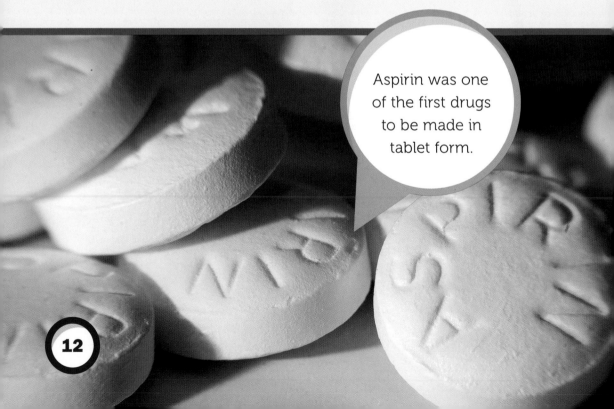

Aspirin was one of the first drugs to be made in tablet form.

reliever in 1900 as aspirin. Now aspirin is the most widely used medicine in the world.

Aspirin works by stopping the body's production of prostaglandin. This chemical makes nerve endings sensitive to pain. Aspirin also lowers fever and swelling. This has made it a common treatment for injuries and for minor illnesses, such as colds and influenza. The pain reliever is used to treat chronic problems, such as arthritis. A low dose taken daily can also reduce the risk of heart attack and stroke in some people.

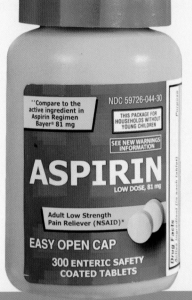

Aspirin has been sold over the counter since 1915.

3,500

Number of scientific articles published about aspirin every year as scientists continue to learn more about its benefits and side effects.

- Aspirin was patented in 1900 by Bayer.
- Used to relieve pain, fever, and swelling.
- Taken in low doses to reduce the risk of heart attack and stroke.

SIDE EFFECTS

Some people have an allergy to salicylates, the chemical found in aspirin and some other products. The side effects can include headache, stomach pain, difficulty breathing, itching, or changes in skin color. People who have these allergies may use other painkillers, such as acetaminophen or ibuprofen.

HYGIENE AND ANTISEPTICS PREVENT INFECTION

Simple hygiene practices such as washing hands can stop the spread of infections. But before the 1800s, doctors did not realize this. They unknowingly spread diseases.

British doctor Joseph Lister started to change this in the 1860s. Working at a university hospital, Lister noticed that many patients survived surgery but died later. Lister had read about other scientists' discovery of microorganisms.

He thought that microorganisms were spreading through the air in the hospital. They entered the body through open wounds to cause infections.

Lister started washing his hands and his tools. He cleaned open wounds and covered them with a cloth soaked in carbolic acid. Carbolic acid had been used to get rid of parasites in livestock. Lister used it as the first antiseptic. An antiseptic

Doctors wash their hands thoroughly and wear face masks to prevent the spread of infections during medical procedures.

46

Percentage of Joseph Lister's patients who died of infections before he started using an antiseptic.

- Infections spread through microorganisms.
- Dr. Joseph Lister started using carbolic acid as an antiseptic in 1865.
- Hygiene and antiseptics still used to prevent infections.

stops the growth of microorganisms on living tissue. The death rate of Lister's patients dropped from 46 percent to 15 percent. Lister retired in 1893. By that time, many doctors were using hygiene and antiseptics to prevent infections.

THINK ABOUT IT

Hygiene isn't just important for doctors. What do you do to help prevent the spread of infections?

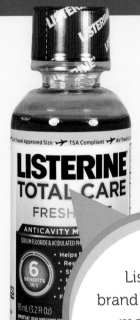

Listerine, a brand of antiseptic mouthwash, was named after Joseph Lister.

GERM THEORY

French scientist Louis Pasteur discovered that milk goes sour because tiny organisms, called microorganisms, multiply in it. He found out that microorganisms also cause other foods and drinks to spoil. Pasteur thought the same thing could happen in the human body to cause diseases. This idea was called "germ theory."

PENICILLIN BECOMES NEW WAY TO SAVE LIVES

In 1942, Connecticut woman Anne Miller was near death. She had blood poisoning after having a miscarriage. Miller was the first patient to receive a new drug called penicillin. She made a full recovery. Finally, doctors had a cure for many deadly infections.

Throughout history, doctors used a kind of mold to fight disease.

Penicillin comes from the mold *Penicillium notatum.*

But they didn't know how or why it worked. Alexander Fleming found some answers. In 1928, the scientist was experimenting with bacteria, a type of microorganism that causes disease. Some mold accidentally spilled into the bacteria culture. Fleming noticed that the bacteria didn't grow where the mold was. Fleming did more experiments and discovered that the mold could kill many types of bacteria.

Other scientists started researching the mold. In 1941, penicillin became

Alexander Fleming discovered penicillin by accident while working in his lab.

1945

Year Alexander Fleming and two other scientists received a Nobel Prize for the discovery of penicillin.

- Alexander Fleming discovered the mold used to make penicillin in 1928.
- Stops the growth of bacteria.
- Led to the discovery of many other antibiotics.

available in drug form. Penicillin became one of the first antibiotics to be widely used. An antibiotic is a medicine that can kill bacteria. Penicillin can be used to treat throat infections, meningitis, and many other infections. The discovery of penicillin led scientists to look for other antibiotics.

X-RAYS LET DOCTORS SEE INTO HUMAN BODY

In 1895, German scientist Wilhelm Conrad Roentgen was experimenting with cathode rays. Cathode rays are a type of electric current sent through a glass tube. Roentgen noticed that the ray made a fluorescent screen in the room glow. The screen glowed even when he put thick black cardboard around the tube. Roentgen didn't know how the rays were getting through the cardboard. So he called them "x-rays."

Roentgen experimented by putting different objects between the tube and the screen. Finally, he put his hand there. He could see the outline of his bones on the screen. The rays were traveling through the fleshy parts of his hand but not through the bones. The screen showed the outline of the bones. Roentgen's discovery would become very useful

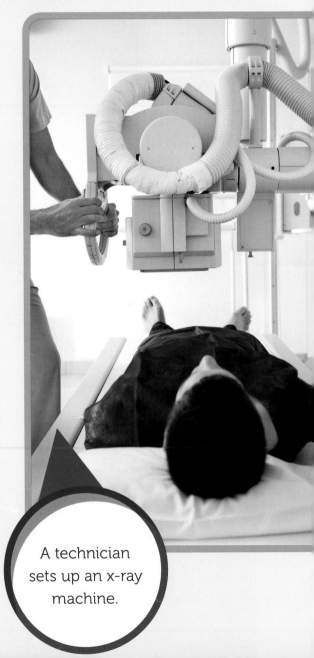

A technician sets up an x-ray machine.

to doctors. They could use the technology to see inside the body.

X-ray machines were first used during World War I (1914–1918). They let doctors see broken bones or bullets that had entered the body. Soon, x-ray machines were being used in most hospitals. At first, the x-rays only let doctors see hard objects, such as bones. Later x-ray machines could be used to see soft tissues, such as organs or blood vessels.

15
Minutes a typical x-ray procedure takes to perform.

- X-rays discovered by Wilhelm Conrad Roentgen in 1895.
- Allows doctors to see inside the body.
- Used to see broken bones, bullets, or swallowed objects.

X-ray images are recorded on special film that is sensitive to the rays.

BLOOD TYPING LEADS TO SAFE TRANSFUSIONS

Accidents or surgery can cause blood loss. Too much blood loss can lead to death. This is why doctors give blood transfusions. Blood that has been donated is given to a patient who needs it. When doctors first tried this, many patients who received donated blood died. Doctors thought some kind of infection caused the deaths.

Austrian scientist Karl Landsteiner had a different idea. In 1901, he discovered that different people have different types of blood. If a person with one blood type is given blood

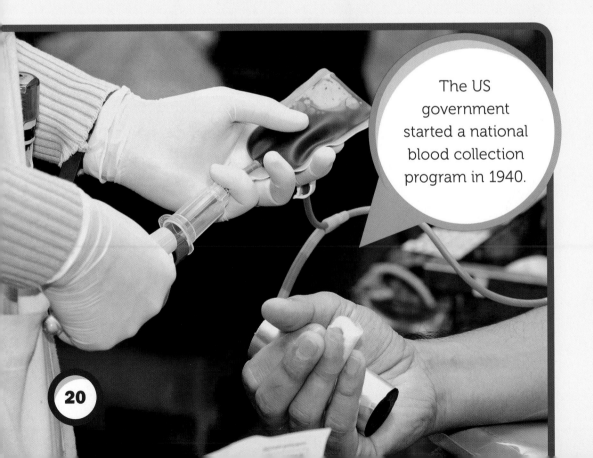

The US government started a national blood collection program in 1940.

12
Number of tests run on donated blood to check for infections.

- Blood typing was discovered by Karl Landsteiner in 1901.
- Explained different types of blood.
- Made blood transfusions safe.

DONATING BLOOD

Most healthy people can donate blood starting at age 17. Approximately one pint (0.5 L) of blood is collected at a time. A person can donate once every eight weeks. Donations are labeled and stored in refrigerators until needed.

from a donor with a different type, it causes a reaction. The body's own immune system attacks the blood cells. The results can be deadly.

Landsteiner developed a system of blood typing to prevent this reaction. Landsteiner's system separates blood into four groups. A patient usually receives blood from a donor with the same type. One type of blood, called O-negative, is safe for anyone. This system was used during World War I. It saved many lives on the battlefield. Now blood transfusions are common in hospitals around the world.

Hospitals keep supplies of different types of blood on hand so they can treat any patient.

ORGAN TRANSPLANTS SAVE LIVES

Richard and Ronald Herrick were twin brothers. In 1954, Richard was dying of kidney disease. He was 23 years old. People have two kidneys but only need one to survive. Ronald agreed to give one of his kidneys to Richard. Dr. Joseph Murray did the surgery. Richard lived for eight more years. This was not the first organ transplant, but it was the first time the patient lived. It proved that organ transplants were possible.

Richard Herrick, *left*, made history when he received a kidney from his twin brother, Ronald, in 1954.

80

Average number of people to receive an organ transplant each day in the United States.

- First successful organ transplant in 1954.
- Donated organs are used to replace organs that are failing.
- Now performed using most vital organs.

THINK ABOUT IT

People can choose to donate their organs when they die. Why would someone want to donate their organs? Why might they not want to?

Most organs can only be stored for a short time before transplant surgery.

The success of that surgery led other doctors to perform kidney transplants. In the 1960s, doctors started performing transplants with other organs. They tried transplant surgeries for the liver, pancreas, heart, and lungs. They used organs from patients who had recently died. Many of these early attempts were not successful. Beginning in the 1970s, success rates improved. Now 80 to 90 percent of organ transplant surgeries are successful.

HUMAN ORGAN
FOR
TRANSPLANT
HANDLE WITH EXTREME
CARE AND KEEP COOL
DO NOT FREEZE

PROSTHETICS PROVIDE BETTER LIMB REPLACEMENT

An estimated 2 million people living in the United States have lost a limb. Artificial limbs, called prosthetics, can help them lead normal lives. Early prosthetics were very basic. They were made out of wood, metal, or leather. Artificial limbs improved in the 1500s. French surgeon Ambroise Paré is considered the inventor of modern prosthetics. Paré designed limbs that were adjustable and movable. He put hinges in prosthetic hands. He made prosthetic knees that could bend and lock.

New materials have made modern prosthetics more lifelike than ever.

Some prosthetic limbs are specially designed for athletes.

45

Percentage of limb losses that occur due to accidents. The rest are caused by diseases.

- Prosthetics were improved by Ambroise Paré in 1536.
- Paré made prosthetics adjustable and movable.
- Modern prosthetics can look and move naturally.

Prosthetics have continued to improve over the years. Modern prosthetics are strong and light. They use materials such as titanium, carbon fiber, and plastics. They can look like a natural body part. Some can move just like an arm or leg. Some have motors that control how they move. Sensors detect slight movement from the user and make adjustments.

12

DNA HOLDS ANSWERS FOR GENETIC DISEASES

Parents hand down traits to their children. These traits can include eye and hair color. They can also include a risk of getting certain diseases. The traits are carried in genes. Genes are carried in DNA, a substance inside the cells of living things.

By the 1950s, scientists knew a lot about how genetics worked. But they did not know what DNA looked

The cells of every living thing contain DNA.

like. Rosalind Franklin was a chemist working in London. She photographed DNA using x-ray technology. Her x-ray images showed the structure of DNA.

In 2003, scientists finished making a map of the entire human DNA strand. They can use the information to study thousands of genes. They can study the genes that increase a person's risk for diseases such as cancer, diabetes, and heart disease. This information may provide tools to combat many complex and serious health problems.

25,000
Approximate number of genes in humans.

- DNA structure photographed by Rosalind Franklin in 1952.
- DNA strand map finished in 2003.
- Scientists can study DNA to learn about genetic diseases.

Researchers at the Cancer Research Institute in Great Britain study the DNA of cancer patients.

FACT SHEET

- Penicillin has saved many lives. But it has become less effective over time. The more it is used, the better bacteria get at resisting it. Now the antibiotic no longer works on some diseases. Doctors have had to use other antibiotics. Bacteria have learned to resist some of these antibiotics, as well. To slow down this trend, many doctors are careful to only prescribe antibiotics when they are really needed.

- Not every illness has a cure. Many viruses, such as the common cold, cannot be cured. Patients with such illnesses can take medicines to treat the symptoms. They can also take care of themselves by getting plenty of rest and drinking fluids.

- Doctors now have many tools to diagnose diseases. Some are special machines. A CT scan uses x-ray technology. It lets doctors view detailed images of organs, bones, or blood vessels. An MRI uses magnetism and radio waves to make images. It can help doctors find a tumor or view damage to an organ.

- A person has to give permission for their organs to be donated before they die. One person can save or improve up to 50 lives by donating his or her organs. Living donors can donate bone marrow, a kidney, a portion of the liver, or skin tissue.

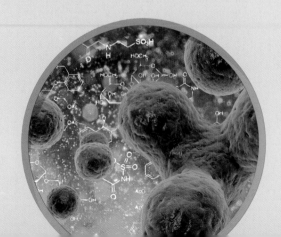

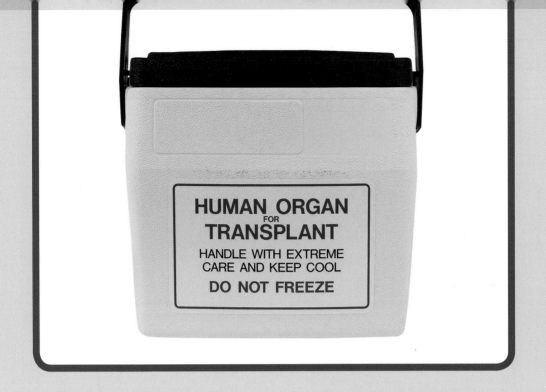

HUMAN ORGAN
FOR
TRANSPLANT
HANDLE WITH EXTREME
CARE AND KEEP COOL
DO NOT FREEZE

- More than 100,000 people are waiting for organ donations in the United States. Eighteen people die every day because they need an organ.

- Vaccines have been developed to protect against many diseases. One of the most serious was polio. In 1952, polio caused approximately 3,000 deaths in the United States alone. It left many other people disabled. Dr. Jonas Salk invented a vaccine for polio in 1953. Since the 1960s, polio has been eliminated from most of the world.

- Medical advancements have increased life expectancy in many parts of the world. In 1900, most Americans could expect to live to be approximately 47 years old. Americans born in 2014 will live an estimated 79 years on average.

GLOSSARY

antibody
A substance produced by the body to fight disease.

antiseptic
A substance that prevents the growth of microorganisms that can cause infection.

artificial
Made by people rather than occurring naturally.

bacteria
Tiny organisms that sometimes cause disease.

diagnose
To find the cause of a problem or to recognize an illness by examining someone.

donor
A person who gives something in order to help someone else.

experiment
A scientific test to learn about something.

genes
Parts of a cell that affect how a living thing grows or appears.

hygiene
Things people do to keep themselves and their surroundings clean, to promote good health.

microorganism
A very small living thing that can only be seen with a microscope.

surgery
Medical treatment where a doctor cuts into a person's body.

transfusion
The transfer of blood into a person's veins or arteries.

virus
A tiny organism that causes a disease.

FOR MORE INFORMATION

Books

Beccia, Carlyn. *I Feel Better with a Frog in My Throat: History's Strangest Cures.* Boston, MA: Houghton Mifflin Harcourt, 2010.

Bredeson, Carmen, and Gerald Kelley. *Don't Let the Barber Pull Your Teeth: Could You Survive Medieval Medicine?* Berkeley Heights, NJ: Enslow, 2013.

Bryant, Jill. *Medical Inventions.* New York: Crabtree, 2013.

Jacobson, Ryan. *Marvelous Medical Inventions.* Minneapolis, MN: Lerner, 2013.

Raum, Elizabeth. *The Cold, Hard Facts about Science and Medicine in Colonial America.* North Mankato, MN: Fact Finders, 2011.

Websites

Kids Health
kidshealth.org/kid

Kids Work!: History of Medicine
www.knowitall.org/kidswork/hospital/history

PBS: Health and Medical Technology
www.pbs.org/topics/technology/health

INDEX

About the Author

M. M. Eboch writes about science, history, and culture for all ages. Her novels for young people include historical fiction, ghost stories, and action-packed adventures.